The
Vile
Files

The Vile Files

Tracey Turner

Illustrated by Chris Fisher

■ SCHOLASTIC

Scholastic Children's Books,
Commonwealth House, 1-19 New Oxford Street,
London WC1A 1NU, UK

A division of Scholastic Ltd
London ~ New York ~ Toronto ~ Sydney ~ Auckland
Mexico City ~ New Delhi ~ Hong Kong

Text copyright © Tracey Turner, 2002
Illustration copyright © Chris Fisher, 2002

ISBN 0 439 97804 1

Contents

Introduction

In this book you'll find lots of things to make you go...

and even...

Read on and discover...

- A truly disgusting rabbit habit
- How to make convincing vomit you can *eat*
- Why bottom burps smell

... and hundreds more horrible facts and disgusting-but-true stories. So if you were hoping for nice facts about flowers, cute pictures of bunnies, and instructions for how to make a pretty friendship bracelet – sorry, but you're in for a big disappointment. That kind of thing is all very well in its place, but this is *The Vile Files* and anything nice has been BANNED from its pages.

As well as finding out all kinds of gruesome information, you can fill in the Vile Things About Me section and keep a file on your family, friends and teachers. There's also a diary and address pages – packed with yet more vile facts – so you'll be able to keep your school timetable and friends' phone numbers in the same place as those all-important reminders of the smelliest plant on earth and which is the best type of cockroach to keep as a pet. You'll wonder how you ever managed without it.

WARNING

Anyone who is easily shocked should read no further.

The
Vile
Files

VILE
THINGS
ABOUT
ME

VILE FACT

Now wash your hands: germs in human poo can pass through ten layers of loo paper.

VILE FACT

Californian Louise Hollis holds the world record for the longest toenails. In 1991 they reached a combined length of 2.17 metres.

VILE FACT

Queen Inez de Castro was crowned in Portugal in 1357. But she had to be dug up to attend the ceremony – she'd been dead for two years.

Me

Name: _Chloe Maily anna gail_
Date of birth: _21/1/2000_
Address: _____

_____

Telephone number: _____
Email: _Alyth primaly s_
School: _Alyth primaly school_

My most horrible habit: _____

_____

Grossest experience: _____

_____

The most vile person I know: _____

My favourite vile fact: _____

_____

_____

My Vile Family

Mums like to pretend they have no disgusting habits, but this is almost never true. Think back over the years: you must have spotted her picking her nose, cutting her toenails in the kitchen or blaming the dog for stinky whiffs.

Mum's name: _Tanya Chir Edward_
Her most horrible habit: _____

You probably have loads to choose from as dads are often very proud of their horrible habits. We've allowed extra space in case you can't decide which one is the most horrible of all.

Dad's name: _Scott James Min_
His most horrible habit: _____

Brothers are famous for many different kinds of vileness. Again, it's likely that you will be spoilt for choice – from runny white puke in the case of baby brothers, to rumbling burps and foul smells of all types in the case of older ones.

Brother's name: *Scott James Min*
His most horrible habit: ....

....

Brother's name (2): ....
His most horrible habit: ....

....

Apart from baby sisters, who are all pretty vile, sisters can be divided into two groups: those who pretend not to have any bad habits at all, and those who delight in acts of vileness.

Sister's name: ....
Her most horrible habit: ....

....

Sister's name (2): _____
Her most horrible habit: _____

Fleas, smells, poo in
unexpected places,
bottom-licking ...
and that's just
brothers and sisters.
For pets, the list is
endless.

Pet's name: Choncho _____
Its most horrible habit: _____

Pet's name (2): Heartley _____
Its most horrible habit: _____

Vile Teachers

Teachers are famous for a wide variety of unpleasant behaviour. The worst offenders might boast bad breath, body odour, suspicious stains on clothing ... or just plain old nastiness to their long-suffering pupils. Fill in the disgusting habits of your teachers here – arrange them in order of vileness – perhaps you could arrange an awards ceremony for the winner (sure to go down well at morning assembly)?

Vilest Teacher of All

Name: ....

Subject: ....

Horrible habits: ....

....

....

....

Vileness rating: 10/10

Runners-up

Name: ....

Subject: ....

Horrible habits: ....

....

....

Vileness rating: ....

Name: ....

Subject: ....

Horrible habits: ....

....

....

Vileness rating: ....

How Vile Are You?

Try this test to discover just how vile you, and your friends and relations, really are...

1. How many of these vile habits do you have?
a) nose picking (award yourself 15 extra points if you eat the bogeys)
b) parping in public
c) nail biting

2. You drip egg yoke on your shirt. Do you...
a) put the shirt in the wash and find a clean one
b) sponge it off with a dish cloth
c) think the colour goes quite well with the tomato sauce you dripped on it yesterday

3. You've slept in the same sheets for a week now. Do you...
a) think they need changing
b) think they'll do for another week or two
c) you don't understand the question

4. When you're told to tidy your room, do you...
a) put books and mags on shelves and generally tidy everything away, then vacuum, dust and polish everything
b) throw out the old yoghurt pots with mould in them and stick everything else in the wardrobe
c) kick things under the bed and hope no one notices

5. How many times a week do you have a bath or shower?
a) seven
b) two
c) a quarter (i.e. once a month)

6. After a meal you should...
a) ask permission to leave the table
b) belch loudly
c) lick the plate and then belch loudly

7. Which of these statements is true?
a) you should always close the lid of the toilet after using it
b) peeing in the shower is normal behaviour
c) pooing in the shower is normal behaviour

8. You notice there is dirt under your fingernails. Do you...

a) think, "Aaarrghhh!" and go and scrub your nails immediately

b) scrape out as much of it as you can with a pointy object

c) do nothing. What's so unusual about that?

9. Which of the following do you think of as normal behaviour?

a) brushing and flossing teeth at least twice a day

b) putting on clean underwear every day

c) washing your hands after every visit to the loo

d) conducting experiments on ancient food in the "lab" under your bed

10. How often do you change your socks?

a) every day

b) every week

c) you only own one pair

Scoring

1. a) 5 (plus possible extra 15)
b) 5 **c)** 2
2. a) 0 **b)** 2 **c)** 5
3. a) 0 **b)** 3 **c)** 10
4. a) 0 **b)** 3 **c)** 5
5. a) 0 **b)** 5 **c)** 10
6. a) 0 **b)** 5 **c)** 10
7. a) 0 **b)** 10 **c)** 50
8. a) 0 **b)** 5 **c)** 8
9. a) 0 **b)** 0 **c)** 0 **d)** 10
10. a) 0 **b)** 15 **c)** 50

If you scored 0 ... you are squeaky clean.

Either that or you're lying. What are you doing reading this book?

If you scored 2-15 ... you have vile potential.

Unless you scored 10 points from **3c)**, **5c)** or **6c)**, in which case you are disgusting.

If you scored 15-30 ... you are fairly foul.

But see above, and add **7b)** and **10b)** to the list.

If you scored 30+ ... you are absolutely vile.

Congratulations!

If you agreed with 7c) ... seek professional help immediately.

The Vile Files

VILE FACT FILE

VILE FACT

You produce two litres of saliva every day – you drink most of it. Thirsty?

VILE FACT

In the Middle Ages, shaving a chicken's bottom and strapping the live bird to a plague sore was believed to be a cure for the Black Death.

VILE FACT

Thomas Crapper did not invent the toilet as many people believe, but with a name like his, he had to be involved in some way: he designed and made toilets in the 19th century. He called one of his toilets "The Deluge"!

Vile People

The Musical Tooter

Believe it or not, at the end of the 19th century, the highest-paid entertainer in the entire world made his living from going on stage and producing parps in front of huge audiences.

Joseph Pujol was born in France in 1857. One day Joseph discovered that he had an unusual ability: he could suck air into his bottom and, by controlling the force with which he released the air, he could produce musical notes. He was soon playing simple tunes using his amazing behind.

Joseph would entertain his school friends with his tuneful bottom. When he joined the army and performed for his mates there, he earned the nickname Le Petomane, which is French for "parp maniac".

Later on, Joseph worked as a music-hall entertainer using his unique wind instrument.

His musical bottom burping was an overnight success. In 1892, performing as Le Petomane, Joseph went on stage at France's top venue – the Moulin Rouge in Paris. His 90-minute show  was so funny that it's said one man died of a heart attack because he was laughing so much. The act included Joseph blowing out candles from huge distances with his amazing bum. Joseph continued to be a very popular entertainer until 1914, when his unusual act lost its appeal.

Mr Methane

Le Petomane's proud tradition lives on: an Englishman known as Mr Methane makes his living in the same bizarre way. Having discovered his amazing ability doing yoga exercises when he was 15, Mr Methane later gave up his job as a train driver to become a full-time bottom-burping entertainer. His live act includes playing tunes and blowing out candles, just as

Le Petomane did 100 years before him. Unlike Le Petomane, however, Mr Methane has also produced a video and CD of his work. He is currently the only person in the world with a career in passing wind.

Four Foul Facts about Bottom Burps

1. Most people parp between 15 and 20 times a day. Everybody does it – even the Queen – so don't believe anyone who claims they don't.

2. On average, an adult man will produce roughly 600 ml of gas from his bottom per day – that's enough to blow up a small balloon!

3. The main reason bottom burps smell is the presence of sulphur. So the more sulphur contained in the food you eat, the smellier your parps will be. Meat and eggs are supposed to be responsible for the smelliest bottom burps – beans and lentils produce lots of parps, but the gas will be less smelly.

4. Holding in a bottom burp is supposed to be bad for you – although there is scientific debate on the subject. The Roman Emperor Claudius believed that this was true, and legalized parping at banquets because he was concerned for his guests' health. Of course, this makes you wonder who banned it ... and why.

Making an exhibition

Vile things are very popular – and so gross exhibitions in art galleries and museums are not uncommon. Here are a few that were shown in 2001/2002:

- The Human Body Exhibition in Chicago, USA, featured a vomit machine and a giant sneezing nose.

- The Wolverhampton Art Gallery showed works of art made from human body fluids.
- To enter the Grossology exhibition at the London Science Museum, visitors went through a giant mouth to find out information about warts, spots, burps and urine.
- An exhibition of 78 different types of human and animal dung was shown at the Tokyo Science Museum in Japan. There was a special section where you could feel the poo.
- A Danish museum put a pooing baby on display at 11:30 every morning – the time when the artist (the baby's father) knew his son normally emptied his bowels.

Head Shrinking

The Jivaro people of the Amazon rainforest are famous for an especially vile reason: they are the only people in the world to have had the horrible habit of chopping off their enemies' heads and then shrinking the heads as trophies of war.

The Jivaro believed that this would stop the spirit of the dead person from taking revenge.

In case you've ever wanted to know, here's how they did it:

How the Jivaro made Shrunken Heads

1. *They killed an enemy in battle and chopped off the head.*

2. *They made a slit in the back of the head and peeled off the skin and hair from the skull. (They threw the skull away – or gave it as an offering to the anaconda god.)*

3. *They sewed the eyes shut and skewered the lips closed with wooden pegs.*

4. *They simmered the head gently for an hour or so, until it was about one third of its original size, but the hair was still attached.*

5. *They sewed up the slit they had made in the back of the head. Now they had something that looked a bit like a deflated football – except a lot more gruesome.*

6. They dropped a hot stone into the head cavity – this made the head shrink even more – and repeated this over the next few days.

7. When the head was small enough – about the size of a man's fist – they moulded it with hot stones to reshape any features that were a bit squished.

8. They hung the finished product over a fire to harden and blacken it.

9. They put some special threads through the lips to finish it off.

10. The head was now ready to be hung around a warrior's neck. Delightful!

The Jivaro people still live in the jungles of Ecuador. But, of course, horrible human head shrinking doesn't happen any more.

VILE FACT

A real shrunken head was bought recently for $10,000.

Disgusting Dinners

Can You Stomach It?

Feeling hungry? If so, be glad you don't have to suffer like Alexis...

In the 1820s, a young Canadian man called Alexis St Martin had a hunting accident that left him with serious injuries including a big hole in his stomach. His doctor, William Beaumont, didn't expect Alexis to live, but amazingly he did ... the only trouble was that the hole in his stomach wouldn't heal.

This meant that Alexis had to bandage his stomach whenever he ate to stop the contents from spilling out. As if that wasn't bad enough, Doctor Beaumont had been watching Alexis's

 progress with great interest, and started performing gruesome experiments on the unfortunate man's open-plan insides. The doctor would do truly vile things like draining Alexis's stomach juices, making him swallow a piece of meat on a string then pulling it out

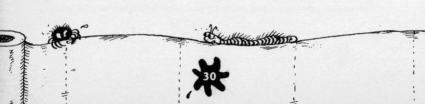

again later to examine it, and sticking thermometers into Alexis's guts.

Doctor Beaumont started following his patient's unique stomach around. This went on for 11 years and, not surprisingly, it got on Alexis's nerves – he had become a walking experiment. But eventually the doctor published a book on what he'd found out from his experiments, complete with gruesome pictures.

Sick to his Stomach

Lazzaro Spollanzani was an 18th-century Italian scientist, who became famous for his work on snails. He regrew their heads and other fascinating (kind of) stuff. He's less well known for the revolting experiments he made ... on puke.

Lazzaro was interested in how food changed once it was inside the body (aren't we all?), and to find out more he forced a variety of different animals to eat food and then sick it up again. It

wasn't long before he moved on from this, and began eating food and then chundering himself. But it gets worse ... Lazarro began eating, puking and then eating the puke, all in the cause of scientific research. He took even this to extremes, and ate some food, barfed, ate the barf, barfed that up, ate the barfed barf, barfed that up, and ate the *barfed barfed barf*.

VILE FACT

Scientist Santorio Sanctorius (1561–1636) also wanted to find out what happens to the food we eat. And his experiments were almost as strange as Lazzaro's: he carefully weighed every morsel of food he ate, then he weighed every morsel of ... erm ... his own poo and wee. He discovered that what came out weighed a lot less than what went in.

Mr Eat Everything

The person with the most famous vile diet must be Monsieur Mangetout. Michel Lotito comes from Grenoble, France and really has earned his nickname (Monsieur Mangetout means Mr Eat Everything). Since 1966, the unfussy eater has managed to chomp his way through:

- 18 bicycles
- 15 shopping trolleys
- 7 TV sets
- 6 chandeliers
- 2 beds
- 1 pair of skis
- 1 coffin
- 1 Cessna

light aircraft

Monsieur Mangetout's unusual diet includes 900 grammes of metal every day.

A 19th-century Oxford University lecturer and all-round nutter, William Buckland, also deserves the same nickname. It seems that nothing was safe with William around. He ate:

- an elephant's trunk
- mice
- bluebottles
- roast giraffe
- a bear that had been advertising a butcher's shop
- the mummified heart of Louis XIV

... but he didn't eat any metal as far as we know.

Insect Eaters

The thought of eating insects might horrify you, but in fact 80 per cent of the world's population eats them. (In fact, everyone does, since insects get ground up and find their way into our food – you can't see them, and they won't do you any harm.) Eating insects is very sensible, as there are so many of them and, if you know the right ones to try, they're tasty and good for you. All over the world, people are chomping on our six-legged friends...

1. Grasshoppers are eaten in Mexico, Africa, many parts of Southeast Asia and Japan. Locusts (really big grasshoppers) are boiled and salted and eaten in Africa.

2. In many countries it's the grub stage of an insect's life that is the most appetising. Witchety grubs (which look like fat white worms) are a traditional Australian Aborigine food – the grubs are gathered from a piece of rotten wood and simply eaten alive. The grub of the huge Goliath beetle is eaten in Africa, caterpillars are munched in Mexico, and in Japan people eat boiled wasp larvae.

3. Termites are roasted and eaten by the handful in parts of Africa – the equivalent of a packet of crisps.

4. Fancy insects on toast? In Columbia, ants are ground up and used to spread on bread.

5. Sago worms – the larvae of beetles – are eaten in Borneo and Papua New Guinea.

6. A can of "mixed insects" is available to buy on the Internet from a Thai company. The

appetising mixture includes crickets and water beetles (which look like giant black cockroaches and are a common food in Thailand).

VILE FACT

If you think eating insects is vile, remember that honey is made from bee spit. Yum.

Maggot Cheese – Don't Try This at Home

Does the thought of eating insects put you right off your cheese on toast? Well, you might be surprised to hear that in many parts of the world people think that eating cheese is pretty vile. And when you consider what cheese is – basically milk  that's gone off, and that lots of different types of cheese have mould growing on them to add to the flavour – it's not difficult to see why. But anyone in their right mind would be revolted by one particular type of cheese...

Maggot cheese is eaten by some strange individuals in Sardinia. It's definitely not one you'll want to try, but here's the recipe anyway:

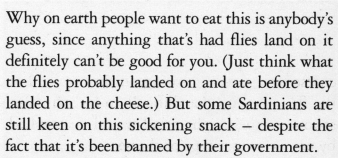

How to make maggot cheese

1. *Take some cheese made from sheep's milk and leave it out in the sun.*

2. *Keep an eye out and you'll see that plenty of flies will land on it and lay their eggs.*

3. *Simply wait for the maggots to hatch.*

4. *Spread the delicious maggotty cheese on some bread and eat it – complete with live maggots. Scrumptious!*

Why on earth people want to eat this is anybody's guess, since anything that's had flies land on it definitely can't be good for you. (Just think what the flies probably landed on and ate before they landed on the cheese.) But some Sardinians are still keen on this sickening snack – despite the fact that it's been banned by their government.

Foul Food Facts

1. Chinese "bird's nest soup" is made from ... birds' nests. The nest of a particular type of swallow is used for the soup. This bird produces a sticky substance (a bit like saliva) to build its nest, which is the special ingredient of the soup.

2. Scotland is well known for haggis – bits of animal innards cooked in a sheep's stomach. Another Scottish national dish is powsowdie – a whole sheep's head, complete with brains, cooked and served in broth.

3. Durians are a fruit that comes from Southeast Asia. The inside of the fruit is very tasty but the outside stinks – apparently it smells like a sewage plant. The smell is so bad that eating durians on public transport is banned in Singapore.

4. Bats, fish eyes and snakes are all on the menu in Southeast Asia.

5. The Japanese puffer fish, or *fugu*, must be the most dangerous dish in the world. Parts of the fish's insides can be poisonous enough to kill you, and yet it's often served in restaurants. Only specially licensed chefs are allowed to prepare it (it takes up to seven years for a *fugu* chef to be trained). Between 100 and 200 people a year are poisoned by *fugu* – about 60 per cent of them die. Although the fish is supposed to taste good, it surely wins the prize for the foulest food?

VILE FACT

In Japan in 2001, a woman found a 4-cm-long dead frog in a custard pudding she'd bought at a supermarket. Fancy a dessert?

Vile Animals

Miracle Mike the Headless Chicken

If you're about to eat your dinner, you might prefer to save reading this next vile story until later...

It's not uncommon for a chicken's body to run around after its head has been chopped off. That's what happened one day in 1945, when a farmer from Colorado in the United States chopped off the head of one of his chickens. But this chicken didn't carry on running around for just a few minutes ... or even hours.

The days went by, and Miracle Mike (as the headless chicken became known) continued to strut about as if having his head cut off was no problem at all. He tried to preen his feathers (pretty unsuccessfully), stood on his perch, and crowed (well, he made a horrible gurgling noise).

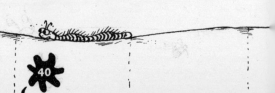

Miracle Mike's fame spread, and soon people were paying money to witness the incredible headless chicken – Mike had laid a golden egg. The farmer fed him by dropping feed down the bird's neck (literally – uuurrrggghh). Amazingly enough, Miracle Mike lived on without his head for a year and a half (although some reports say he survived headless for four years). Experts at the time said that the farmer had made a bit of a hash of chopping off Mike's head, and had left enough of the brain stem for the chicken to function almost normally. They also said that Mike wasn't suffering without his head ... which seems a bit hard to believe.

Miracle Mike lives on: his home town of Fruita, Colorado, stages an annual event in his honour, where people play games like "Pin the head on the chicken" and "Run like a headless chicken". You can buy Headless Mike T-shirts, too.

Awful Animal Facts

1. Flamingos have a vile way of cooling down: they pee down their legs.

2. When camels get angry (which is quite a lot) they puke up some half-digested food and spit it at whatever, or whoever, they're annoyed with.

3. Cute little bushbabies wee on their paws, leaving foul-smelling prints wherever they go. So remember – never shake hands with a bushbaby.

4. Lots of animals eat their own sick or feed it to their babies. But the frigate bird makes other birds throw up and then eats *their* chunder.

5. Rabbits and baby elephants both eat their own poo.

6. Hippos splatter their dung all over the place by twirling their tails round while they're pooing. They do this to spread their scent – which must make them popular.

7. Skunks are famously foul-smelling: the animal sprays a disgustingly smelly yellow liquid which can travel nearly five metres. Humans can  smell a skunk a mile away – literally.

8. Cows produce 450 litres of wind per day.

9. Dogs sometimes eat the poo of other animals – probably because of the vitamins or protein it contains. Or maybe because they're just vile.

10. Tamandua anteaters are known as "Stinkers of the Forest" because of their appalling pong.

Creepy, Crawly and Slimy

Spider Surprise

The biggest spider in the world is the Goliath Tarantula (also known as the Goliath Birdeater). The creature's leg span can measure up to 30 cm (urrrggh.) The spider doesn't eat birds, but prefers insects, toads, mice, small snakes and

lizards. Don't expect to find one lurking under your bed, though – the Goliath is only found in northern South America.

If the thought of a huge, hairy spider that's bigger than a dinner plate makes you shudder, you might be surprised to hear that the Piroha tribespeople in Venezuela collect Goliath Tarantulas. Then they eat them, roasted, avoiding the poison and fangs. The spiders are taken along on hunting trips as a sort of packed lunch. (Be glad the next time you end up with peanut-butter sarnies.) The spiders even come complete with built-in toothpicks – the Piroha tribe use the spiders' fangs to pick their teeth clean when they've finished eating their meal.

You might also be surprised to hear that tarantulas, including the Goliath, are often kept as pets – what could be cuter? Thankfully, despite being the world's biggest spider, the Goliath Tarantula's poison isn't strong enough to kill you, and if you were bitten by one it wouldn't be serious.

Dung of Desire

You've probably heard of dung beetles. They begin their dungy lives by hatching out from eggs inside a big ball of manure. Then they turn into larvae, and the ball of dung becomes their food supply. Mmmm.

As adults, the beetles feed on ... more dung. The adult males make a big ball of dung (up to the size of an apple) to attract a female — the female will only be interested in really  impressive balls of manure (wouldn't you be?).

Then the female lays her eggs in the dung ball, and the whole process starts again.

The beetles, which are most commonly found in Africa, eat the dung of plant-eating animals.

Most animals only use some of the goodness in the food they eat, so their poo is full of yummy wholesome goodness (erm, and a lot of unwholesome, un-yummy bacteria) — and the dung beetle is specially adapted to be able to eat it and use the larger animals' left-over food. Isn't nature wonderful?

Big Bug Facts

1. Goliath beetles are the heaviest flying insect in the world. In Senegal, children often keep them as pets.

2. Stick insects can be up to 36 cm long.

3. The heaviest insect on record was a Giant Weta from New Zealand, which weighed in at 71 grammes.

4. The bulkiest insect is the Acteon Beetle, which comes from South America. It can be up to 9 cm long, 5 cm wide and 4 cm thick.

Insect Pets

Have you ever asked yourself, "What's the best kind of cockroach to keep as a pet?" Well, apparently it's the Giant Hissing Cockroach — sounds really cute, doesn't it? Up to 7.5 cm long,

these creatures don't have wings and don't carry germs like other cockroaches, which is why they make such good pets. (Yeah, right.) They really do hiss, which must be especially appealing.

VILE FACT

Flies barf and then eat it. It helps their digestion.

Learn to Love a Leech

You might think leeches are vile. It's true that they have three mouths and millions of teeth, they're slimy, they suck people's blood and they're not very

pretty. But look at the plus side: leeches come complete with their own anaesthetic, so a leech bite is painless – you won't even know a leech is gorging itself on your blood (up to five times its own body weight) until you see it. And they're only small, so they're hardly going to kill you. (Well, most of them are small – the longest leech on record was 45 cm long.)

In days gone by, doctors were very keen on attaching leeches to their patients in order to "bleed" them – which quite often did more harm than good. But leeches have made a comeback in medicine, and this time they're actually useful: they're used in surgery because they produce a chemical which stops blood from clotting.

So the next time you see a leech having a snack at your expense (leeches are found in most parts of the world), don't leap up and down shouting "Aaarrggghh!" – leave it to finish its meal, when it will drop off naturally with no harm done.

VILE FACT

Most spiders' fangs aren't big or strong enough to break human skin, so most of them can't hurt us. The Brazilian Huntsman spider is thought to be the most poisonous in the world, but another strong contender for the world record is the Sydney Funnel Web.

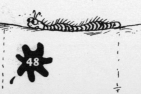

How Vile Are You? (part two)

It's quiz time again and another chance for you to find out just how vile you are. How many of these queasy-making quiz questions can you answer correctly?

1. Bearing in mind that humans parp on average 16 times a day, how many times a day do cows pass wind?
a) 32 times
b) 100 times
c) 300 times

2. Whole roasted guinea-pigs are eaten as a delicacy in which country?
a) France
b) Australia
c) Peru

3. Do you practise onychophagia?
a) Yes, and I've got really good at it.
b) No.
c) How dare you! That's disgusting.

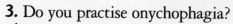

4. The Sydney Funnel Web is the very poisonous spider that we met on page 48. Its fangs are strong enough to bite through...

a) A pair of cotton shorts

b) A human fingernail

c) Steel

5. If a cockroach gets its head chopped off, what happens?

a) It dies

b) It runs around like a headless chicken for a few minutes and then dies

c) It lives for a week or so and then dies

6. Which of these might you find on the menu in Canada?

a) Seal-flipper pie

b) Moose mousse

c) Snow-goose stew

7. What happens if you swallow chewing gum or bubble gum?
a) It gets stuck inside your stomach for ever, forming a big ball of gum
b) Nothing – it comes out like any other waste product
c) Your poo becomes stretchy

8. Entomophagy is the posh word for...?
a) Bottom burping
b) Eating insects
c) Earwax

9. What is black pudding made from?
a) Mince meat
b) Blood
c) Dough mixed with squid ink

10. How fast does food travel through your guts?
a) 1.5 metres an hour
b) 20 metres an hour
c) 5 metres an hour

Scoring

Award yourself two points for every question you answered correctly:
1. – c) Phew; **2. – c)**; **3. – a) b)** and **c)** Oncychophagia means biting your nails, so all the answers could be right – give yourself two points anyway; **4. – a)** and **b)**; **5. – c)** Cockroaches can survive for a more than a week without their heads before dying of starvation; **6. – a)** Seal-flipper pie is eaten in Newfoundland, Canada; **7. – b)**; **8. – b)**; **9. – b)**; **10. – a)**.

If you scored 2-6 ... you are a vile-fact innocent.
This isn't very impressive – especially considering you were given two points for question three.
If you scored 8-12 ... you are a vile-fact novice.
You could be well on your way to being the sort of person who has a vile fact at their fingertips for every occasion.
If you scored 14-20 ... you are a vile-fact champion.
Congratulations – how did you do it? (By looking at the answers?)

The
Vile
Files

VILE
JOKES

VILE FACT

Burping is just the way you get rid of the air you've swallowed with your food – the quicker you eat, the more you talk while eating, the more fizzy drinks you have, and the more you chew gum, the more you'll burp.

VILE FACT

The South American golden arrow frog has the deadliest poison in the world. The frogs are only 2-3 cm long, yet the poison from just one frog could kill almost 2,000 people.

VILE FACT

The first toilet paper was sold in 1880 – before that people used all kinds of things, including moss, bunches of herbs, leaves and even goose feathers.

What's green and red and spins at 100 mph?
A frog in a blender.

"Mum? What happened to all that food Tiddles wouldn't eat?"
"Shut up and eat your meatloaf."

What's yellow and smells of bananas?
Monkey sick.

"Mum? What's a vampire?"
"Shut up and drink your soup before it clots."

What's black and white and red all over?
A penguin in a blender.

How do you keep flies out of the kitchen?
Put a big pile of manure in the living room.

What has a hazlenut in every bite?
Squirrel poo.

"Mum? I keep running round in circles!"
"Shut up, or I'll nail your other foot to the floor."

What's a fly's favourite chat-up line?
"Is this stool taken?"

What has four legs and an arm?
A happy Rottweiler.

What rushes out of the ground shouting, "Bottom burps!"
Crude oil.

What's white on the outside, yellow on the inside, and wriggles?
A maggot sandwich.

A Sick Joke

Barfing, puking, chundering, multi-coloured yawning ... whatever you call it, a good bit of vom in the right place is guaranteed to turn everyone green. The recipe for this fake chunder couldn't be simpler – but you might have to practise your method before you really fool anyone. Once you've got your act off to a fine art, take heed of the warning at the end...

You will need:
a can of extra thick vegetable soup
a straight face
convincing puking noises

Method:
1. Open the can of soup and put some in a container.
2. Complain of feeling sick to parent/other victim of sick joke. Rush off in direction of bathroom.
3. Grab your carefully and handily hidden container of soup. Scatter soup about in style of horrifying projectile vomit. (Tip: only spill the soup on to lino or tiled surfaces so that it's easy to clean up.)

4. Make horrendous barfing noises.
5. Stand in bathroom clutching stomach and looking deathly, as the victim of your joke starts screaming and runs to phone doctor.
6. Laugh uproariously.
7. Receive long talking-to and spend half an hour cleaning up soup. Laugh quietly anyway at memory of victim's horrified face.

WARNING

Make sure you don't let your victim continue thinking you really have puked all over the bathroom for too long or they may well faint/be REALLY angry/call the doctor before you can stop them.

If you have a pet, you could pretend the fake sick is theirs. When your victim notices the chunder, go over to it and stick your finger in it. Eat a bit of it, saying, "Yeah, Tiddles is always doing that, but in fact it doesn't taste too bad!" Your victim will be completely grossed out.

What's white on the outside, green on the inside and hops?
A frog sandwich.

Why do gorillas have such big nostrils?
Have you seen the size of their fingers?

What do you give an elephant with an upset stomach?
Plenty of room.

What do you call a person covered in cow dung?
Pat.

What do you call a man with a spade in his head?
Doug.

Mum? What's a werewolf?
Shut up and finish combing your face.

What do you get if
you sit under a cow?
A pat on the head.

What has four
wheels and flies?
*A lorry-load of
manure.*

What happens when a
member of the Royal
Family burps?
A royal pardon is issued.

Why did the boy hide
under the bed?
He was a little potty.

What type of nut
do you find down
the toilet?
A peenut.

The
Vile
Files

VILE
DIARY

VILE FACT
Australian Randy Jones has a vile collection of over 2,000 scabs!

VILE FACT
Throughout history there have been lots of cases of disgusting things raining from the sky: in Gloucestershire in 1987 there was a rainfall of pink frogs; sand eels rained on Hendon, London in 1918; it rained herrings in Argylshire in 1871.

VILE FACT
A housefly can smell a piece of meat from seven kilometres away.

Important dates

JANUARY  

1	2	3
4	5	[illegible]
7	8	9
10	11	12
13	14	[illegible]

VILE FACT OF THE MONTH

Fluid from a sneeze can travel more than three and a half metres.

FEBRUARY

1 **2** **3**

4 **5** **6**

7 **8** **9**

10 **11** **12**

13 **14** **15**

VILE FACT OF THE MONTH
Tiny eight-legged mites live in your eyelashes –
they look a bit like crocodiles when you look
at them through a microscope.

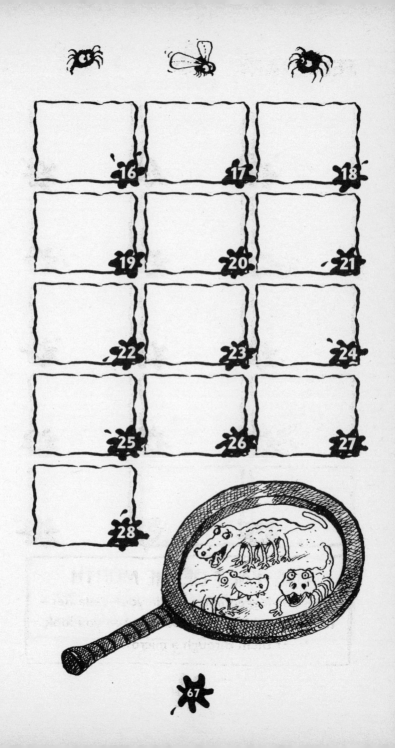

16

17

18

19

20

21

22

23

24

25

26

27

28

MARCH

1

2

3

4

5

6

7

8

9

10

11

12

13

14

15

VILE FACT OF THE MONTH

A Scottish woman has 462 body piercings, 192 of
them on her head. She holds the world record.

APRIL

1 2 3

4 5 6

7 8 9

10 11 12

13 14 15

VILE FACT OF THE MONTH
In 2001, doctors in Berlin, Germany, found a
2.5-cm-long earwig living in a woman's ear.
Did you just hear a scratching noise?

MAY

1 2 3

4 5 6

7 8 9

10 11 12

13 14 15

VILE FACT OF THE MONTH
A French company has invented a special
material that soaks up sweat and disguises
body odour for up to a month. Hurray – only
12 baths a year from now on!

JUNE

1

2

3

4

5

6

7

8

9

10

11

12

13

14

15

VILE FACT OF THE MONTH
Most of the dust in your house is tiny bits of skin shed by you and the rest of your family.

JULY

1

2

3

4

5

6

7

8

9

10

11

12

13

14

15

VILE FACT OF THE MONTH

A type of tapeworm, which can live inside
humans, has been known to reach 18 metres
in length.

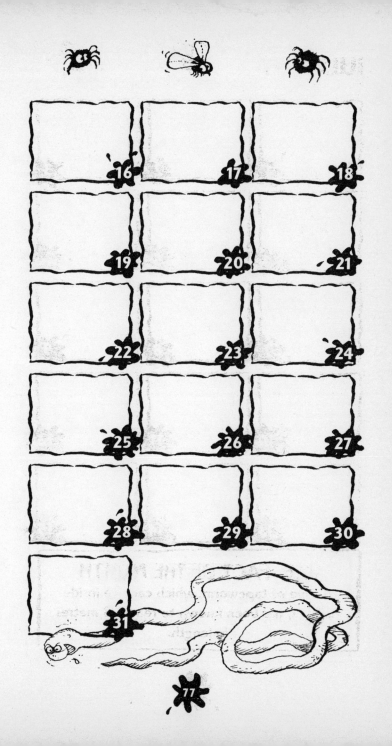

AUGUST

1	2	3
4	5	6
7	8	9
10	11	12
13	14	15

VILE FACT OF THE MONTH
The medical term for nose-picking is
rhinotillexomania – impress your teachers with
your amazing vocabulary!

SEPTEMBER

1	**2**	**3**
4	**5**	**6**
7	**8**	**9**
10	**11**	**12**
13	**14**	**15**

VILE FACT OF THE MONTH
In October 2001, a Manchester woman bit on a biscuit ... and made the vile discovery that it contained a human tooth, complete with a filling. Urrggghh.

OCTOBER

1 2 3

4 5 6

7 8 9

10 11 12

13 14 15

VILE FACT OF THE MONTH
The world's longest fingernails belong to an
Indian man, Shridhar Chillal. The total length of
the fingernails on his left hand was measured at
6.05 metres. He hadn't cut them for 43 years!

NOVEMBER

1 2 3

4 5 6

7 8 9

10 11 12

13 14 15

VILE FACT OF THE MONTH
The "corpse flower" smells like rotting flesh.
It is the smelliest plant on Earth – you can
catch its vile pong over 800 metres away.

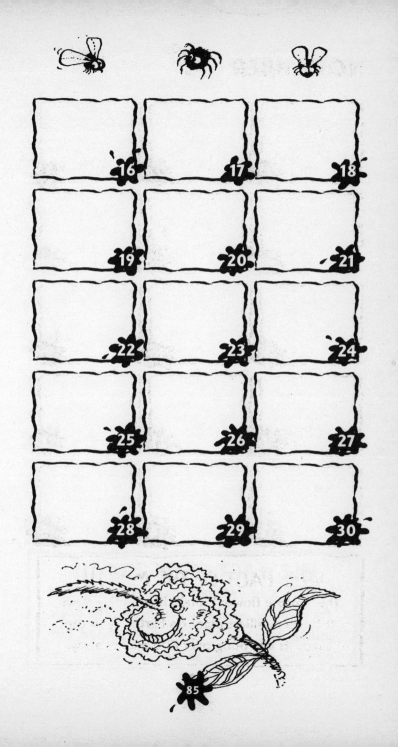

DECEMBER

1

2

3

4

5

6

7

8

9

10

11

12

13

14

15

VILE FACT OF THE MONTH

In 2001, a 16-year-old Spanish boy was fined for breaking wind at a policeman. The boy's mother said that he had indeed parped, but wasn't aiming at the policeman.

Vile school timetable

	a.m.	lunch	p.m.
Monday			
Tuesday			
Wednesday			
Thursday			
Friday			

The
Vile
Files

VILE
ADDRESSES

VILE FACT

In 1987, an 11-year-old girl from Azerbaijan swallowed a poisonous snake ... and lived to tell the tale. The creature snaked into her mouth while she was asleep and the girl woke up choking. But after drinking lots of salt water, she vomited the snake up – and she was fine.

VILE FACT

Environmentally friendly paper can be made from elephant dung. It takes one kilo of dung to make 60 A4 sheets of paper. Apparently the trained eye can tell the age of the elephant and what it's been eating by examining the dung paper.

VILE FACT

Swallowing lice in beer was a Tudor cure for jaundice – it didn't work.

Name: --

Address: --

Telephone: --

Mobile: ---

Email: --

Vileness rating: --

VILE FACT

Cows drop "country pancakes" an average of
16 times a day.

Name: --

Address: --

Telephone: --

Mobile: ---

Email: --

Vileness rating: --

Name: ....

Address: ....

....

....

Telephone: ....

Mobile: ....

Email: ....

Vileness rating: ....

VILE FACT

24 per cent of people admit that they don't
always flush the toilet.

Name: ....

Address: ....

....

....

Telephone: ....

Mobile: ....

Email: ....

Vileness rating: ....

Name: --
Address: ---

Telephone: ---
Mobile: --
Email: ---
Vileness rating: -----------------------------------

VILE FACT

Maggots are used in medicine because they eat
the dead flesh on wounds.

Name: --
Address: ---

Telephone: ---
Mobile: --
Email: ---
Vileness rating: -----------------------------------

Name: ....

Address: ....

....

Telephone: ....

Mobile: ....

Email: ....

Vileness rating: ....

```
┌─────────────────────────────────────────┐
│              VILE FACT                     │
│  A bar in Dawson City in Canada makes a   │
│  special cocktail that is not for the      │
│  faint-hearted: instead of an olive or a   │
│  cherry in your drink you get a pickled    │
│  human toe – yes, a real one. Urrggghh.    │
└─────────────────────────────────────────┘
```

Name: ....

Address: ....

....

Telephone: ....

Mobile: ....

Email: ....

Vileness rating: ....